JOURNAL

OF THE

GENERAL COUNCIL

OF THE

INDIAN TERRITORY,

COMPOSED OF

DELEGATES DULY ELECTED FROM THE INDIAN TRIBES LEGALLY RESIDENT THEREOF.

ASSEMBLED IN COUNCIL

AT OKMULGEE, IN THE INDIAN TERRITORY,

UNDER THE PROVISIONS OF THE TWELFTH ARTICLE OF THE TREATY MADE AND CONCLUDED AT THE CITY OF WASHINGTON, IN THE YEAR 1866, BETWEEN THE UNITED STATES AND THE CHEROKEE NATION, AND SIMILAR TREATIES BETWEEN THE UNITED STATES AND THE CHOCTAW AND CHICKASAW, MUSKOKEE, AND SEMINOLE TRIBES OF INDIANS, OF THE SAME DATE.

SR Scholarly Resources Inc.
1508 Pennsylvania Avenue · Wilmington, Delaware 19806

SCHOLARLY RESOURCES, INC.
Wilmington, Delaware • London

Reprint edition published in 1975

Library of Congress Catalog Card Number: 75-3700
ISBN: 0-8420-1890-5

Manufactured in the United States of America

JOURNAL

OF THE

GENERAL COUNCIL

OF THE

INDIAN TERRITORY,

COMPOSED OF

DELEGATES DULY ELECTED FROM THE INDIAN TRIBES LEGALLY RESIDENT THEREOF.

ASSEMBLED IN COUNCIL

AT OKMULGEE, IN THE INDIAN TERRITORY,

UNDER THE PROVISIONS OF THE TWELFTH ARTICLE OF THE TREATY MADE AND CONCLUDED AT THE CITY OF WASHINGTON, IN THE YEAR 1866, BETWEEN THE UNITED STATES AND THE CHEROKEE NATION, AND SIMILAR TREATIES BETWEEN THE UNITED STATES AND THE CHOCTAW AND CHICKASAW, MUSKOKEE, AND SEMINOLE TRIBES OF INDIANS, OF THE SAME DATE.

LAWRENCE:
EXCELSIOR BOOK AND JOB PRINTING OFFICE.
1871.

JOURNAL.

OKMULGEE, Tuesday,
September 27, A. D. 1870.

Council convened at 9.30 A. M.

Superintedent Enoch Hoag presiding.

J. G. Vore, Secretary *pro tem.*

Credentials of members of different tribes presented, and the following delegates admitted to seats:

CHEROKEE NATION, -	Wm. P. Ross.
	Riley Keys.
	Allen Ross.
MUSKOKEE NATION, -	G. W. Stidham.
	Pleasant Porter.
	John R. Moore.
	L. C. Perryman.
	G. W. Greyson.
	Joseph M. Perryman.
	Sanford W. Perryman.
OTTAWAS, - - -	Francis King.
EASTERN SHAWNEES, -	Lazarus Flint.
QUAPAWS, - - -	George Lane.
SENECAS, - - -	James King.
WYANDOTTES, - -	James Hicks.

CONFEDERATE PEORIAS, &c.,	Edward Black.
SAC AND FOX, - -	Keokuk.
	Mut-ta-tah.
ABSENTEE SHAWNEES, -	John White.
	Joseph Ellis.

A quorum not being present,

Council adjourned until 2 o'clock P. M.

TWO O'CLOCK P. M.

Council met pursuant to adjournment.

Credentials of members presented, and the following delegates admitted to seats:

CHEROKEE NATION, -	S. H. Benge.
MUSKOKEE NATION, -	Oktars-har-sars Harjo, of Arpe-kar.
	Cot-cho-che, of We-wo-ka.
CHEROKEE NATION, -	John Sarcoxie.
GREAT AND LITTLE OSAGES,	Augustus Captain.
	Wm. Connor.

A quorum not being present,

On motion, Council adjourned until 9 o'clock A. M., to-morrow.

WEDNESDAY, Sept. 28, 1870,
9 O'CLOCK A. M.

Council met pursuant to adjournment.

Credentials of members presented, and the following delegates admitted to seats:

CHEROKEE NATION,	-	O. M. P. Brewer.
		J. A. Scales,
		S. M. Taylor.
		Stealer.
MUSKOKEE NATION,	-	Timothy Barnard.

On motion, an informal committee of five was appointed to report upon the organization and order of business for the General Council.

Committee:—W. P. Ross, P. Porter, F. King, S. H. Benge, A. Captain.

A quorum not being present,

On motion, Council adjourned until 2 o'clock P. M.

TWO O'CLOCK P. M.

Council met pursuant to adjournment.

Report of informal committee received.

On motion, action was deferred until a quorum should be present.

A quorum not being present.

On motion, Council adjourned until 9 o'clock A. M., to-morrow.

THURSDAY, Sept. 29, 1870,
9 O'CLOCK, A. M.

Council met pursuant to adjournment.

Credentials presented and the following delegates admitted to seats:

MUSKOKEE NATION,	-	J. M. C. Smith.
CHEROKEE NATION,	-	Moses Alberty.
		Ezekiel Proctor.
		Joseph Vann.
GREAT AND LITTLE OSAGES,		Wah-tah-in-kah.

A quorum being present, Council proceeded to business.

Preceding minutes read and adopted.

Report of informal committee submitted for action.

REPORT.

The committee on the order of business, report and recommend,

1st. That the provisions of the twelfth article of the treaty of August, 1866, between the United States and the Cherokee Nation, be adopted as the present basis of the power and duties of General Council of the Indian Territory.

2d. That a majority of delegates entitled to seats in the General Council, shall be necessary to constitute a quorum for the transaction of business, but a less number during a lawful session thereof may adjourn from day to day and adopt such measures as may be deemed necessary to compel the attendance of absent members.

3d. There shall be elected by the General Council, a Secretary, whose duties shall be such as are defined by Treaty.

4th. There shall be elected in like manner, one Doorkeeper, whose duty shall be prescribed by order of the President.

5th. That a committee of seven members be appointed by the President to report rules for the government of the Council in the transaction and order of business.

6th. That there shall be appointed by the President the following standing committees for the session, whose duty it shall be to consider and report by bill or otherwise upon subjects that may be referred to them by order of the Council, to wit:

1st. A Committee on Relations with the United States.

2d. A Committee on International Relations.

3d. A Committee on the Judiciary.

4th. A Committee on Finance.

5th. A Committee on Education and Agriculture.

6th. A Committee on Enrolled Bills

J. R. Moore offered the following amendment:

In first paragraph after the words "General Council of the Indian Territory," insert "nor shall said Council legislate on matters pertaining to the organization, laws, or customs of the several tribes."

Amendment lost.

Report of the committee adopted.

On motion, election of Secretary was deferred until Monday, Oct. 3d.

Robert Carr was duly elected Doorkeeper.

The following Standing Committees were appointed by the President:

Committee on Relations with the United States.—W. P. Ross, S. H. Benge, G. W. Stidham, S. W. Perryman, and L. Flint.

Committee on Internal Relations.—Allen Ross, P. Porter, Francis King, Keokuk, Augustus Captain, J. A. Scales, and J. R. Moore.

Committee on Judiciary.—Riley Keys, G. W. Stidham, S. M. Taylor, Edward Black, and Augustus Captain.

Committee on Finance.—J. A. Scales, Moses Alberty, J. M. Smith, L. C. Perryman, and John White.

Committee on Education and Agriculture.—J. M. Perryman, O. H. P. Brewer, Joseph Vann, Tim. Barnard, Wm. Connor, J. M. C. Smith, and W. P. Ross.

Committee on Enrolled Bills.—W. P. Ross, J. A. Scales, and J. M. Perryman.

Committee on Rules for the government of the Council in the transaction and order of business.—W. P. Ross, G. W. Greyson, G. W. Stidham, R. Keys, F. King, and G. Lane.

On motion, Council adjourned to meet at 2 o'clock P. M.

TWO O'CLOCK P. M.

Council met pursuant to adjournment.

Credentials presented and the following delegates admitted to seats.

SEMINOLE NATION, - Fus-hat-che Harjo.
John F. Brown.

On motion the following resolutions were adopted:

Resolved, That the Committee on Education be instructed to report in writing, as near as may be practicable, the population of the nations and tribes represented in the General Council, the amount of their respective school funds, the number of schools in operation among them, the system under which they are managed and the general state of education in the Indian Territory.

Resolved, That the Committee on the Judiciary be instructed to report a bill or bills which shall provide for the arrest and extradition of criminals and offenders escaping from one tribe to another tribe, and for the administration of justice between members of different tribes of the Indian Territory, and persons other than Indians and members of said tribes and nations.

Resolved, That the Committee on Internal Relations be instructed to report a bill or bills to regulate matters pertaining to the intercourse and relations of the Indian tribes and nations resident in the Indian Territory.

Report of Committee on Rules for the government of the Council in the transaction and order of business received and adopted.

REPORT.

In order to expedite and conduct the proceedings of the present Council with some regard to the rules governing other similar assemblies, the committee appointed for that purpose would respectfully recommend the adoption of the following rules for the government of the Council now assembled at Okmulgee, C. N., agreeable with treaties of 1866, in the transaction and order of business, to wit:

1st. That the Council shall meet daily (Sunday excepted) at 9 o'clock A. M., unless otherwise ordered by the Council.

2d. When called to order by the President, it shall be the duty of the Secretary to call the roll and read the journal of the preceding session.

3d. All propositions and motions, before being acted upon, shall be duly interpreted to all the tribes present.

4th. Voting on all propositions shall be done by raising the right hand, but the *ayes* and *nays* shall be taken and duly recorded by the Secretary when it is so desired by ten members.

5th. Any member wishing to make a motion or discuss a proposition, shall arise to his feet and address the presiding officer as "Mr. President," and confine himself to the subject under consideration and abstain from all remarks of a personal or offensive character. Any member transgressing the foregoing rule shall be called to order by the presiding officer, and not be allowed to proceed without his consent.

6th. No motion shall be entertained by the Council unless such motion shall have been seconded.

7th. All bills and resolutions requiring the action of the Council, shall be reduced to writing and read three several times before being acted upon.

8th. The style of the action of the Council shall be, "Be it enacted (or resolved) by the General Council of the Indian Territory.

9th. A motion to adjourn shall at all times be in order.

On motion, Council adjourned until 9 o'clock A. M., to-morrow.

FRIDAY, Sept. 30, 1870,
9 O'CLOCK A. M.

Council met pursuant to adjournment.

Preceding minutes read and adopted.

Committee on Education and Agriculture asked for and was granted further time.

Committee on Judiciary asked for and was granted further time.

On motion, the following resolution was adopted:

Resolved by the General Council of the Indian Territory, That the Committee on Relations with the United States be instructed to report a memorial to the Pesident of the same, setting forth our relations with the General Government, as defined by treaty stipulations, and protesting against any legislation by Congress impairing the obligation of any treaty provision, and especially against the creation of any government over the Indian Territory, other than that of General Council; and also against the sale or grant of any lands, directing or contingent upon the extinguishment of the Indian title, to any railroad company or corporation now chartered for the purpose of constructing a railroad from a point north to any point south, or from a point east to any point west, through the Indian Territory, or the construction of any other railroad, other than those authorized by existing treaties.

On motion, Council adjourned until 2 P. M.

TWO O'CLOCK P. M.

Council met pursuant to adjournment.

Clement N. Vann, delegate from the Cherokee Nation, admitted to a seat.

A communication from the Principal Chief of the Choctaw Nation to Superintendent E. Hoag, was submitted, in which he stated that no delegates to the General Council had been elected or appointed, and no provisions made authorizing him to do so; also one from the authorities of the Chickasaw Nation, stating that owing to the shortness of time from the reception of notice, until the meeting of this Council, it would be impossible for the representatives of that nation to be present at that meeting of the Council, but that they would attend at as early a day as possible.

On motion of C. N. Vann, the following resolutions were unanimously adopted:

Resolved by the General Council of the Indian Territory, That the nations, parties to the treaties of 1866, making provisions for the organization of this Council, hold that in good faith they are bound by those provisions.

Resolved further, That it is the sense of this Council that any nation, party to the treaties referred to, or included within the provisions, *are* and *ought to be* bound by the authority and action of this Council, whether they send delegates to, or participate in its deliberations or not.

On motion, Council adjourned until 7 o'clock P. M.

SEVEN O'CLOCK P. M.

Council met pursuant to adjournment.

Credentials presented and the following delegates admitted to seats:

CHEROKEE NATION, - Stand Waitie.

On motion, the following resolutions were presented and unanimously adopted:

Whereas, The short notice given of the convening of the General Council of the Indian Territory, has prevented the attendance of delegates from some of the nations entitled to representation in the same, therefore,

Be it Resolved by the General Council of the Indian Territory, That when this Council adjourns to-day, it will be to meet again at 10 A. M., at this place, on the first Monday in December next, unless otherwise ordered by the Secretary of the Interior.

Resolved, That the standing committees appointed under the rules of the Council, be continued and instructed to report in full upon the several subjects referred to them at that time by order of the Council.

Resolved, That the Secretary be requested to furnish a copy of these resolutions to the executives of the Choctaw and Chickasaw Nations, and request the attendance of delegates from their nations, at the adjourned sessions of the General Council of the Indian Territory.

On motion the following resolutions were unanimously adopted:

Resolved by the General Council of the Indian Territory, That there be conveyed to the Comanche, Kiowa, Arapaho, Cheyenne, Coddo, Wichita, and other tribes of Indians living on the Plains, assurances of friendship and kind feelings of the nations represented in this General Council, and an expression of their earnest wish that relations of peace may be established between them and all men, of whatever race or color.

Resolved further, That Ok-tar-har-sars-Harjo be authorized and requested by the General Council to convey the foregoing resolutions to said Indians, and to earnestly invite them to meet us in Council, at our session in December next.

On motion, the Secretary was requested to send a transcript of the resolutions to said Indians, with names of all the delegates at this Council attached, designating the tribes to which they belong.

On motion, the following resolution was adopted:

Resolved, That the Committee on Education and Agriculture be instructed to report fully, as may be practicable, upon the condition of agriculture in the Indian Territory, including the area of land in cultivation, the crops produced, the different plants and cereals adapted to the climate and soil, and the best methods of cultivating such crops, and of increasing the industry of the people in agricultural pursuits.

C. N. Vann was added to the Committee on Relations with the United States, Committee on the Judiciary, and Committee on Enrolled Bills.

John F. Brown was added to the Committee on Relations with the United States, and Committee on Enrolled Bills.

On motion, Council adjourned.

[Signed.] ENOCH HOAG,
Pres't and Sup't of Indian Affairs.

J. G. VORE, *Secretary.*

JOURNAL.

OKMULGEE, M. N., Tuesday,
December 6, A. D. 1870.

General Council of the Indian Territory assembled pursuant to adjournment.

Enoch Hoag, Superintendent of Indian Affairs, presiding.

J. G. Vore, Secretary *pro tem.*

Delegates present:

CHEROKEE NATION, -	O. H. P. Brewer.
	S. M. Taylor.
	J. A. Scales.
	Stealer.
	Joseph Vann.
MUSKOKEE NATION, -	Geo. W. Stidham.
	John R. Moore.
	G. W. Greyson.
	Joseph M. Perryman.
	Timothy Barnard.
OTTAWAS, - - -	Francis King.
CONFEDERATE PEORIAS, &c.,	Edward Black.

Credentials presented, and the following delegates admitted to seats:

CHOCTAW NATION, -	Campbell Leflore.
	John McKinney.
	Wm. Fry.
	Ma-ha-tubbe.
	Alexander R. Durant.
	James Thompson.
	Joseph P. Fulsom.
	Alfred Wright.
CHICKASAW NATION, -	Charles P. H. Percy.
	Joseph James.
	Hopiah-tubbee.

A quorum not being present,

On motion, Council adjourned until 9 o'clock A. M., to-morrow.

WEDNESDAY, Dec. 7, 1870,
9 O'CLOCK A. M.

Council met pursuant to adjournment.

The following delegates took their seats:

MUSKOKEE NATION, -	L. C. Perryman.
	Sanford W. Perryman.
	Oktar-har-sars Harjo.
CHEROKEE NATION, -	John Sarcoxie.
GREAT AND LITTLE OSAGES,	Augustus Captain.
SEMINOLE NATION, -	John F. Brown.
	Fus-hat-che Harjo.

On motion, the following resolution was unanimously adopted:

Resolved, by the General Council of the Indian Territory, That the following delegates be added to the several committees: Alfred Wright, on Relations with the United States.

James Thompson, on Judiciary.

Campbell Leflore and J. P. Folsom on International Relations.

John McKinney, on Education and Agriculture.
C. P. H. Percy, on Finance.

A quorum not being present, Council adjourned until nine o'clock A. M. to-morrow.

THURSDAY, Dec. 8, 1870,
9 O'CLOCK A. M.

Council met pursuant to adjournment.

Geo. W. Walker was admitted to a seat, as delegate from the Muskokee Nation.

A quorum being present, Council proceeded to business.

On motion, the following persons were appointed by the President to interpret the proceedings of the General Council, to the members of the different nations who do not understand the English language:

For the Muskokee and Seminole Nations, David M. Hodge.

For the Choctaw and Chickasaw Nations, Joseph P. Folsom.

For the Absentee Shawnees, Robert Deer.

The delegate from the Muskokee Nation, to whom was committed the message and invitation to the Comanche, Kiawa, Arapaho, Cheyenne, Caddo, Wichita and other tribes on the plains, reported the message and invitation had been transmitted through the interpreter for the Absentee Shawnees, and that no response had as yet been received.

Credentials of members presented, and the following delegates admitted to seats:

SENECAS, George Spicer, in place of James King.

WYANDOTTES, George Wright, in place of James Hicks.

The journal of the first session of the General Council read and explained.

Mr. Percy, delegate from the Chickasaw Nation, submitted the following additional rule for the government of the Council in the transaction and order of business, which was adopted:

RULE 10.—The General Council, when a quorum is present, shall be the judge of the legal qualifications of its own members. For this purpose it shall have power to examine into the validity of the credentials of its members, determine the eligibility of contestants and claimants for seats, or it may refer the same to a Committee on Credentials. The Committee on Credentials shall have all the available power to cause persons or papers, or certified copies thereof, to be brought before it, and shall make a correct report of the investigations and conclusions to the General Council for its final adjudication, in all matters pertaining to the legal qualifications and eligibility of members from the several nations of the Indian Territory, whose seats may be contested.

On motion, Council adjourned until 2 o'clock P. M

TWO O'CLOCK P. M.

Council met pursuant to adjournment.

Credential presented by George W. Johnson, from the Cherokee Nation, who was admitted to a seat.

The following delegates from the Cherokee Nation took their seats:

Moses Alberty, Ezekiel Proctor.

The following Committee on Credentials was appointed by the President:

J. R. Brown, Muskokee Nation; C. P. H. Percy, Chickasaw Nation; James Thompson, Choctaw Nation; Francis King, Ottawa Nation; J. A. Scales, Cherokee Nation; J. F. Brown, Seminole Nation; Keokuk, Sac and Fox Nation; G. W. Walker, Muskokee Nation.

On motion, credentials of Locher Hayo, Charke and Thlathlo Yoholo were referred to the Committee on Credentials.

Committee on Education and Agriculture was called upon for a report. A part of the committee being absent a report was deferred.

Mr. Leflore, delegate from the Choctaw Nation, submitted the following resolution:

Resolved by the General Council of the Indian Territory, That the President be, and is hereby, authorized to appoint a committee of ten, to devise a permanent organization of the Indian Territory as contemplated in the treaties of 1866, with the several tribes resident in the said Indian Territory. Adopted.

The following committee was appointed:

Campbell Leflore, Choctaw Nation; W. P. Ross, Cherokee Nation; C. P. H. Percy, Chickasaw Nation; G. W. Greyson, Muskokee Nation; J. F. Brown, Seminole Nation; Edward Black, Confederate Peorias, &c.; Francis King, Ottawa Nation; Augustus Captain, Osage Nation; Geo. Spicer, Seneca Nation; J. A. Scales, Cherokee Nation.

Council adjourned until 9 o'clock A. M., to-morrow.

FRIDAY, Dec. 9, 1870,
9 O'CLOCK, A. M.

Council met pursuant to adjournment.

Preceding minutes read and adopted.

Credentials presented and the following delegates admitted to seats:

CHICKASAW NATION, - Colbert Carter.
Jackson Kemp.

Chairman of the Commitee on Permanent Organization reported progress.

Committee on the Judiciary asked the privilege of deferring a report until after the Special Committee on Organization made a report. Which was granted.

Colbert Carter, of the Chickasaw Nation, was placed upon the Committee on Permanent Organization.

J. A. Scales, of the Cherokee Nation, was placed upon the Committee on the Judiciary, vice Clement N. Vann, resigned.

Mr. Wm. P. Ross, delegate from the Cherokee Nation, informed the Council that Henry Chambers had been appointed by the authorities of said nation, to fill the place of C. N. Vann resigned, and that the delegate was present, ready to take his seat, but without his credentials, which had not as yet reached him.

On motion it was referred to the Committee on Credentials.

In order that the Committee on Permanent Organization might have time to mature a report, the Council adjourned until 9 o'clock A. M. to-morrow.

SATURDAY, Dec. 10, 1870,
9 O'CLOCK A. M.

Council met pursuant to adjournment.

Preceding minutes read and adopted.

Committee on Credentials submitted the following report:

REPORT.

We, the Committee on Credentials, appointed to examine into the credentials of Locher Hayo and Thlathlo Yoholo, submit the following report:

Upon examination of the credentials of the above named gentlemen, we find that they are so defective and imperfect, and without the signature of any officer of the Muskokee Nation, authorized to commission members of the Council, that we cannot recognize them as being sufficient to entitle the claimants to seats in the General Council of the Indian Territory.

The credentials of Charke having been examined, we find that he has been substituted by Cot-cho-che, the former incumbent, to take his place on account of inability to discharge his duties as a member, caused by sickness. The substitution has been approved by the Executive of the Muskokee Nation, as the credentials will show.

Therefore, we recommend that Charke be allowed to take his seat during the present session of the Council, agreeable to the approval of the credentials.

In the case of Mr. Chambers, from the Cherokee Nation, the committee find from information deemed reliable, that Mr. Vann has resigned his seat in this Council, and that Mr. Chambers has been appointed by the authority of that nation, to fill the vacancy, and is therefore, in the opinion of your committee, entitled to his seat in the General Council of the Indian Territory.

[Signed.] JAMES THOMPSON,
Chairman Committee.

Attest: CHAS. P. H. PERCY,
Clerk Committee.

On motion, the report of the Committee on Credentials was adopted, and Charke of the Muskokee Nation, was admitted to a seat during the present session of the General Council.

Henry Chambers was admitted to a seat as a delegate from the Cherokee Nation, in the place of Clement N. Vann resigned.

Joseph James, of the Chickasaw Nation, was placed on the Committee on Education and Agriculture.

Colbert Carter, of the Chickasaw Nation, was placed upon the Committee on the Judiciary.

Report of the Special Committee on Permanent Organization submitted:

REPORT.

The Special Committee, to whom was assigned the duty of making a report upon the resolution of the General Council, in the words following, to wit:—

"*Resolved by the General Council of the Indian Territory*, That the President be, and is hereby, authorized to appoint a committee of ten, to devise a permanent organization of the Indian Territory, as contemplated by the treaties of 1866, with the several tribes resident in the said Territory"—respectfully state that they have given the subject such consideration as was in their power. They regard the organization of the Indian Territory, under any form of government, as of the gravest importance to all the people who inhabit it.

The large and invaluable interests in lands and money, which belong to the nations and tribes who are settled therein; the provisions of their several treaties with the United States; their distinct form of government and franchise, arising under them; their different languages and diversified conditions, present severally and combined interests not to be too lightly estimated, nor too hastily disposed of, in arranging the terms of any organization that may be designed to blend in one harmonious system the whole of them, at the same time that it preserves a just and impartial regard for their respective rights.

The opposition of all Indians to any form of territorial government that has been proposed by the Congress of the United States, is too notorious to require any comment. It is firmly and ineradicably imbedded in their very nature. They cling to their homes, to their laws, to their customs, to their national and personal independence, with the tenacity of life itself. In these sentiments your committee fully concur. And while the leading powers invested in this General Council pervade, all the treaties negotiated in 1866 by the United States with the different nations here represented, each one of them grants some important concession, or retains some important right not to be found in others. In some respects they merely shadow dimly the duties of this Council, instead of clearly defining its powers and authority. The responsibility of inexperienced legislators, instead of being simplified by them, is made more difficult and complex. As the best means of removing these obstacles, observing a fair deference to the sentiments of our people, and at the same time of preserving our race, and of perpetuating unimpaired the rights of all, the weak and the strong, those less advanced, and those who have made further progress towards civilization, your committee are of the opinion that the organization of the people here represented, and such as may hereafter unite with them, should be a government of their *own choice.* It should be Republican in form, with its powers clearly defined, and full guarantees given for all the powers, rights and privileges respectively, now reserved to them by their treaties. They, therefore, respectfully recommend that the Council proceed to form a constitution for the Indian Territory, which shall conform to existing treaty stipulations, provide for an Executive, Legislative and Judicial Department, and vested with such powers only as have been conceded to this General Council, and not inconsistent with all the rights reserved to each nation and tribe who were parties to the treaties of 1866, and, also, with the final provision that such constitution shall be obligatory and binding only upon such nations and tribes as may hereafter duly approve and adopt the same.

Council adjourned until 9 o'clock A. M., Monday.

MONDAY, Dec. 12, 1870.
9 O'CLOCK A. M.

Council met pursuant to adjournment.

Credentials presented and the following delegate was admitted to a seat:

CHOCTAW NATION, - Coleman Cole.

Minutes of the preceding meeting read and approved.

Report of the Special Committee on Permanent Organization was taken up.

On motion, it was agreed that when a vote should be taken on the adoption of the report on permanent organization, the ayes and nays should be recorded.

The question being upon the adoption of report of Special Committee, the roll was called with the following result:

Ayes—W. P. Ross, Keys, A. Ross, Sarcoxie, Brewer, Taylor, Scales, Vann, of Cherokees; Stidham, Porter, Moore, L. C. Perryman, Greyson, J. M. Perryman, S. W. Perryman, Ok-tar-har-sars Harjo, Charke, Barnard, Smith, Walker, of Muskokees; King, of Ottawas; Flint, of Eastern Shawnees; Spicer, of Senecas; Wright, of Wyandottes; Black, of Confederate Peorias and others; Keokuk and Mut-ta-tah, of Sacs and Foxes; White and Ellis, of Absentee Shawnees; A. Captain, Hardrope, Bevanew, of Osages; Fus-hat-che Harjo, Brown, of Seminoles; Leflore, McKinney, Fry, Ma-ha-tub-bee, Durant, Thompson, Folsom, Wright, Cole, of Choctaws; Percy, James, Hopiah-tubbe, Carter, Kemp, of Chickasaws—48.

Nays—Stealer, Alberty, Proctor, Chambers and Johnson, of the Cherokees—5.

The report was adopted.

On motion of Mr. Carter, of the Chickasaw Nation, the following committee of twelve was appointed to draft a constitution:

COMMITTEE.

W. P. Ross, Cherokee Nation; Campbell Leflore, Choctaw Nation; Colbert Carter, Chickasaw Nation; John F. Brown, Seminole Nation; Francis King, Ottawa Nation; Joseph P. Folsom, Choctaw Nation; G. W. Johnson, Cherokee Nation; C. P. H. Percy, Chickasaw Nation; Ok-tar-har-sars Harjo and G. W. Stidham, Muskokee Nation; Riley Keys, Cherokee Nation; Augustus Captain, Osage Nation.

Council adjourned until 2 o'clock P. M.,

TWO O'CLOCK P. M.

Council met pursuant to adjournment.

The following resolution was submitted by Mr. Smith, of the Muskokee Nation, and on motion of Mr. Ross, unanimously adopted:

WHEREAS, The members of the General Council of the Indian Territory have had the honor to receive Messrs. Campbell, Lang and Farwell, of the United States Indian Commission, and to hear their views in regard to the general interest of the Indians in the Indian Territory, and the expression of their sympathies for the welfare of all the red people; and,

WHEREAS, This General Council is desirous of preserving upon the journal of their proceedings a record of this event in their history, and of their heartfelt appreciation of the noble sentiments of truth, justice and humanity, entertained by the Commissioners; therefore,

Be it Resolved, That the General Council of the Indian Territory hereby record this declaration of the pleasure they have experienced from the attendance upon the Council of Messrs. Campbell, Lang and Farwell, of the United States Indian Commission, of their grateful appreciation of the words of hope, cheer and encouragement they have heard from them, and of their own desire to conform, as far as practicable, with the just and humane policy of the United States, the preservation of peace and kindness between the Indians of this Territory themselves, and with the whites upon their border, and for the improvement and perpetuation of their own people and race.

The report of the Committee on Agriculture was submitted and adopted. [See appendix marked "**A.**"]

On motion, the report was adopted.

On motion, Council adjourned until 9 o'clock A. M., to-morrow.

TUESDAY, Dec. 13, 1870,
9 O'CLOCK A. M.

Council met pursuant to adjournment.

Mr. E. J. Brown, delegate from the Seminole Nation, admitted to a seat.

Preceding minutes read and approved.

The President introduced the Hon. Eli S. Parker, Commissioner of Indian Affairs, who delivered an address setting forth his views as to the wishes and expectations of the government of the United States, and of the friends of the Indians throughout the same, from this General Council of the Indian Territory, with suggestions as to the best mode of legislation to meet those expectations: and also words of cheer and encouragement in this great and important undertaking.

On motion, Council adjourned until 2 o'clock P. M.

TWO O'CLOCK P. M.

Council met pursuant to adjournment.

On motion of Mr. W. P. Ross, the committee of twelve for drafting a constitution for the government of the Indian Territory, retired from the Council for the purpose of entering upon their duties, and was instructed to report at as early an hour as possible.

Committee on Education was granted leave to retire to mature their report.

On motion, Council adjourned until 9 o'clock A. M., to-morrow.

WEDNESDAY, Dec. 14, 1870,
9 O'CLOCK A. M.

Council met pursuant to adjournment.

Preceding minutes read and adopted.

On motion, Mr. Scales, delegate from the Cherokee Nation, submitted a resolution relating to the tribes of the plains.

Referred to the Committee on International Relations.

The Superintendent read the commission assigning to duty G. W. Greyson as Secretary of the General Council of the Territory.

On motion of Mr. Porter, of the Muskokee Nation, the following resolution was unanimously adopted:

Be it Resolved, That the thanks of the General Council of the Indian Territory be and is hereby tendered to J. G. Vore for the able and efficient manner in which he has conducted the duties of the office of Secretary of the Council, and that the President of the Council be instructed to compensate him for his services.

On motion of Mr. Folsom of the Choctaw Nation, the Council adjourned to meet at 9 o'clock to-morrow morning.

THURSDAY, Dec. 15, 1870,
9 O'CLOCK A. M.

Prayer by Mr. Duncan.

Mr. Wm. P. Ross of the Cherokee Nation, announced that there were present two delegates from the Cherokee Nation, who would present their credentials, whereupon Messrs. J. W. Adair and Joseph Thompson presented their credentials and were admitted to seats.

Credentials were also presented by two additional members from the Muskokee Nation, namely: Martup Yoholar in the place of G. W. Greyson resigned, and David M. Hodge in place of D. N. McIntosh, absent.

Minutes of the preceding day were read and adopted.

S. W. Perryman of the Creek Nation, introduced a resolution providing for a committee of three persons, whose duties will be to revise and rearrange the minutes and proceedings of the Council preparatory to printing and publishing the same.

Mr. Moore of the same nation, moved to amend the resolution so as to provide for the re-reading of the same before the adjournment of the present Council.

Resolution as amended was adopted.

Resolution read as follows, namely:

Resolved, That the President be authorized to appoint a committee of three persons to revise and prepare for publication the journal of the proceedings of this General Council, to be read in presence of the Council before its adjournment.

President announced as members of the Committee on Revisions,

Allen Ross of the Cherokee Nation, G. W. Walker of the Muskokee Nation, E. J. Brown of the Seminole Nation.

By request of Mr. Moore of the Muskokee Nation, Mr. James Thompson of the Choctaw Nation was added to the Committee on International Relations.

On motion of J. M. Perryman of the Muskokee Nation, the Council adjourned to meet again at 2 o'clock P. M.

TWO O'CLOCK P. M.

Council met pursuant to adjournment.

The President added to the Committee on Revision, Mr. Joseph Thompson of the Cherokee Nation.

Allen Ross of the Cherokee Nation, chairman of the Committee on International Relations, submitted the report of that committee in the form of a reslution tendering to the wild tribes of the plains the hand of friendship, and recommending to them the prudence of refraining from acts of hostility among themselves, as well as against the citizens of the United States.

The President highly recommended the spirit of the report, and expressed a desire that every effort will be made to better the condition of the tribes of the plains as well as all other Indians.

On motion of J. A. Scales of the Cherokee Nation, the report was unanimously adopted.

Your committee, to whom was referred the resolution in regard to the various tribes of the plains, respectfully state that they have carefully considered said subject, and beg leave to submit the following resolution, and recommend that it be adopted by the General Council:

RESOLUTION IN RELATION TO THE TRIBES OF THE PLAINS.

Resolved by the General Council of the Indian Territory, That the Superintendent of Indian Affairs be, and he is hereby, requested to convey, through their respective agents or otherwise, to the Comanches, Kiowas, Cheyennes, Arapahos, and other tribes of the plains, the fact that the Choctaws, Chickasaws, Cherokees, Muskokees, Seminoles, Osages, Senecas, Shawnees, Ottawas, Peorias, Wyandottes, Quapaws, and Sacs and Foxes, have met in general council and confederated; that the object of this confederation is to preserve peace and friendship among themselves, with all other red men, and with the people of the

United States; to promote the general welfare of all Indians and to establish friendly relations with them; to secure our lands exclusively to ourselves and to transmit them to our children after us; that the nations above named extend to them the hand of friendship; that they earnestly recommend them to refrain from acts of hostility among themselves and with the people of the United States; and that we offer them our aid and council in establishing permanently friendly relations with the Government of the same, and will meet them in council whenever practicable, and desired by the Superintendent of Indian Affairs.

On motion of Porter of the Muskokee Nation, Council adjourned to meet at 9 o'clock to-morrow.

DECEMBER 16th, 1870, }
9 o'clock A. M. }

Council met pursuant to adjournment.

Minutes of the preceding day read and adopted.

Robert Lumbard, as a delegate from the Quapaw Nation in place of Geo. Lane, presented his credentials and was admitted to a seat in the Council.

James M. C. Smith, chairman of the Committee on Education, presented the report of that committee, which was read and referred back to the committee for correction.

On motion of J. R. Moore Council adjourned to meet at 1 o'clock P. M.

ONE O'CLOCK P. M.

President announced that the Committee on the Constitution had reported only a portion of its work, which was taken up, read twice, and interpreted.

The report of the Committee on Education was received as corrected, read, and interpreted; which, on motion of J. M. C. Smith, was laid on the table.

And the report of the Committee on the Constitution was taken up, read and interpreted.

Council adjourned to meet at 9 o'clock to-morrow morning.

SATURDAY, Dec. 17, 1870.

Council met pursuant to adjournment.

Roll was called.

Another portion of the report of the Committee on the Constitution was read and interpreted.

The report of the Committee on the Populations and Educational Interests of the several nations represented in the General Council, was read and adopted. See appendix marked "C."

Smith, of the Muskokee Nation, moved to adjourn until 9 o'clock Monday morning.

Motion sustained.

MONDAY, Dec. 19, 1870,
9 O'CLOCK, A. M.

Council met pursuant to adjournment.

The roll was called by the Secretary.

Mr. Ross, of the Cherokees, introduced the following resolution, which was adopted:

Resolved, That the President of the General Council be respectfully requested to allow the mileage of those members, for the distance they traveled in going to and returning from the regular session of the Council in September last, but who failed to reach it before its adjournment until December.

By order of the President the entire constitution, as drafted by the committee, was read a second time and interpreted.

The Committee on Education submitted a revised copy of their report of the day previous, which was read and adopted.

On motion of C. Leflore the Council adjourned to meet at 2 o'clock.

TWO O'CLOCK P. M.

Council met pursuant to adjournment.

The roll was called by the Secretary.

W. P. Ross, of the Cherokees, introduced an invitation from the Cherokee Council for the location of the capital at Fort Gibson.

Motion by Mr. Ross to lay the same on the table. Motion adopted.

Constitution, as drafted, was put upon its third reading.

Section 6th, of the Declaration of Rights, amended by Percy by inserting after the word *jury*, the words, *of the district wherein the crime shall have been committed*. Amendment adopted.

Mr. Ross moved to amend the 2d section of the 3d article, by inserting after the last word the words, *and for the Sacs and Foxes one Senator*. Adopted.

Mr. Percy, of Chickasaw Nation, moved to strike out the whole section 2d of article 3d, and insert, *The Senate shall be composed of one member from each nation adopting this constitution*.

The ayes and nayes were called for by Geo. W. Johnson, of the Cherokee Nation.

Rejected—nays 48, ayes 8.

Geo. W. Johnson moved to amend by inserting in the 3d section of the 4th article the words, *and who shall not be a natural born citizen of the Indian Territory*.—Withdrawn.

Leflore moved to insert as a part of section 11th of article 4th, the clause, all commissions shall be "In the name and by the authority of the Indian Territory. and be sealed with the seal, and signed by the Governor and attested by the Secretary of the Territory." This clause was adopted.

Mr. Johnson, of the Cherokee Nation, moved to amend the schedule by inserting, "*Provided*, That this constitution shall be obligatory and binding only upon such nations and tribes as may hereafter duly approve and adopt the same." Amendment adopted.

Council adjourned to meet at 9 o'clock A. M., to-morrow.

TUESDAY, Dec. 20, 1870,
9 O'CLOCK A. M.

Council met pursuant to adjournment.

Roll called.

Minutes read and adopted.

Mr. Ross, of the Cherokee Nation, moved to transpose the last clause of the 3d section of the 5th article, and make it the concluding clause of the 1st section of the same article. Adopted.

C. Leflore submitted an additional section as section 17th to the 3d article of the constitution, as follows:

Sec. 17. The salaries of all officers created under this constitution, not otherwise provided, shall be regulated by law, but no increase or diminution shall be made in the same during the term for which said officers may have been elected or appointed.

Adopted.

Mr. J. Thompson, of the Choctaws, moved to amend the schedule by inserting after the words *Councils* in the 8th line, the words, *or the people*. Adopted.

Leflore moved to amend section 9th of article 4th by inserting, *and fines* after the words *respites*.

Adopted.

Mr. Johnson, of the Cherokee Nation, submitted resolutions providing for the submitting of the constitution to the several nations, without taking a vote on the same at the present time, as an amendment to the schedule resolution.

Mr. Scales moved to lay on the table. Motion prevailed.

Mr. Ross called for the ayes and nayes, when votes stood as follows:

Ayes—W. P. Ross, R. Keys, A. Ross, J. Sarcoxie, O. H. P. Brewer, S. M. Taylor, J. A. Scales, Stealer, Moses Alberty, J. Vann, G. W. Johnson, J. Thompson, J. W. Adair, G. W. Stidham, P. Porter, J. R. Moore, L. C. Perryman, J. M. Perryman, Octar-harsars-Hayo, Charke, T. Barnett, J. M. C. Smith, G. W. Walker, Martup Yoholar, D. M. Hodge, C. Leflore, J. McKinney, Wm. Fry, Ma-ha-tubbe, A. R Durant, J. Thompson, J. P. Fulsom, Alfred Wright, Colman Cole, Hopiah-tubbee, C. Carter, J. Kemp, F. King, L. Flint, R. Lumbard, Geo. Spicer, Geo. Wright, Ed. Black, Keokuk, John White, J. Ellis, A. Captain, S. Bavenew, Hard Rope, Wah-ta-in-ka, Fushutche Hayo, E. J. Brown—52

Nays—E. Proctor, H. Chambers, S. W. Perryman—3.

Constitution was declared adopted. [See appendix marked "B."]

O. H. P. Brewer, of the Cherokees, submitted resolutions providing for the sending of delegates to the seat of the United States Government.

On motion of J. Thompson, of the Cherokee Nation, Council adjourned until 2 o'clock P. M.

TWO O'CLOCK P. M.

Council met pursuant to adjournment.

The following resolution was adopted:

Resolved, That the General Council adjourn this day, December 20th, at 3 o'clock, to meet on the first Monday of June, 1871, at Okmulgee, Creek Nation.

On motion of Mr. Ross, of the Cherokee Nation, a unanimous vote of thanks was awarded the President for the impartial and dignified manner in which he has presided over the sessions of the General Council.

On motion of Porter, of the Creeks, a unanimous vote of thanks was also awarded Ed. Earle, Thomas Miller and Dr. Nicholson, for their kind attention and advice during the session of the Council.

On motion of C. Leflore, the Council adjourned to meet at Okmulgee, C. N., on the first Monday in June, 1871.

ENOCH HOAG,
Supt. Indian Afairs,
President Gen'l Council.

G. W. GREYSON,
Secretary.

APPENDIX.

A.

The committee to whom the duty was assigned of reporting upon the agricultural interests and resources of the Indian Territory, regret to say that they have no data upon which to estimate, even approximately, the quantity of land in cultivation within the limits of the Indian Territory.

The Creeks, Cherokees, Choctaws, Chickasaws, Seminoles, Shawnees, Delawares, Senecas, Quapaws, Ottawas, Wyandottes, and the confederated Peorias, Weas, Piankeshaws, and Kas-kas-kias, are an agricultural people and rely upon the cultivation of the soil and the raising of stock for their livelihood, and the Sacs and Foxes, Osages, and others, are making commendable progress in that direction. The extent of their farms vary from a few acres to two and three hundred, and in one instance in the Chickasaw Nation, in the fertile valley of the Washita, to more than two thousand acres. While there are many farms sufficiently large, the majority of them might be increased with great advantage. The interest in this respect is growing, and since the close of the war to the present time, there is a marked progress in the general improvement, in the buildings and farms among the

Indian people. In these respects, there is wide room for further advancement, and this we confidently expect to witness, whenever the constant agitations in Congress and elsewhere, which so much disturb the security of the people and discourage all their efforts to improvement, shall cease.

But notwithstanding all adverse influences, the condition of the people is not stationary, but progressive. The idea which obtains to a considerable extent, in even otherwise well informed circles remote from the homes of the Indians, that they live by hunting, fishing and trapping, is entirely erroneous so far as applied to the nations and tribes enumerated above. They are settled and not nomadic in their habits, and rely upon the cultivation of the soil for their subsistence. Their advancement is not all that we could desire, but is an earnest of better things in the future, and shows a susceptibility for further improvement, and with proper efforts, the native ability to reach a genuine civilization. A large area of the inhabited portion of the Indian Territory is well adapted to the use of improved agricultural implements. Their introduction, as yet, is limited, but perhaps equal to what should be expected when it is borne in mind how much men are apt to do as their fathers did before them, as their neighbors do around them, and as the limited means at their disposal allowed. Reapers, mowers, and threshers of different patents, are seen in some places, while improved plows for turning prairie land and working crops, are found in large numbers. We would desire to impress the people of the Territory engaged in agriculture, with the importance of giving more attention to this subject, than is now done. Good implements, well and timely used, lighten the burdens of labor, impart a real pleasure to employment and largely increase its results. They relieve both man and beast, and directly increase the value of time by increasing its results. The crops which can be profitably grown in the soil and climate of the Territory, are very nearly all those adapted to a rich soil and temperate latitude. Corn is the staple crop, and even under our somewhat defective plan of culture, yields upon an average from thirty to sixty bushels per acre. In favorable seasons it does well in all portions of the Territory. Wheat s not so generally grown as it should be, chiefly, we apprehend, because of the scarcity of mills for the manufacture of flour. The Cherokees, perhaps, grow more than any nation in the Territory. The average yield is about fifteen bushels. It has been known to yield as high as forty-two. But few farmers there, however, prepare the soil and seed it down with the care the crop demands. South of the Canadian, and on the Arkansas and Red Rivers, and the uplands intervening, cotton was formerly extensively cultivated, and was the most valuable crop of that region. We hope yet to see it again whitening large and well tilled fields, and bringing in treasure and wealth to our brothers of the Choctaw and Chickasaw Nations—the Chickasaw crop this year being estimated at five thousand bales. Tobacco is extensively grown.

Of the grasses, we need say but a word. Our prairies furnish all that is now to be had, and all that seems to be cared for. Clover and timothy do well, and would even now repay their cultivation. Blue grass also succeeds well, and will be as much at home in some portions of the Territory as it is in Kentucky. Rye and oats do well all over the Territory, so far as your committee are advised—a species of the former being indigenous to the soil and affording excellent winter pasturage. Potatoes, beans, beets, pumpkins, upland rice, turnips, cabbage, onions, and nearly all garden vegetables in suitable soil and with seasonable culture, grow to perfection. In horticulture, with some exceptions, we are lamentably behind the times. So far as tested, no finer apples are grown in the United States than some we have seen from orchards in the Indian Territory north of the Canadian and Arkansas Rivers. Peaches, pears, plums, and cherries succeed, while the smaller fruits, such as strawberries, raspberries, blackberries, and grapes, are to the "manor born."

Your committee would be much gratified to be the means of awakening a general interest upon this subject, and stirring up the people more generally to the cultivation of the more desirable kinds of fruits. There is pleasure in the pursuit, and health and profit in the results of horticulture.

As regards the domestic animals of the Territory, we need scarcely remark that stock raising must furnish occupation for a large number of our people. It is adapted to their habits, and to our climate, and will be the source of the largest profit to those who embark in it. The number of domestic animals and the quality of their breeds, have been sadly reduced and deteriorated by the war. Large and magnificent herds of cattle have entirely disappeared from our prairies, and the accumulation of forty years vanished into nothingness. But the grass still grows and the waters run, inviting and urging our people to untiring efforts to renew their herds of cattle, horses and hogs, and flocks of sheep and goats. Money, food, and raiment, stimulate them to start again in pastoral life, and to get the best improved breeds of all kinds of stock that may be within their means.

In conclusion, your committee beg leave to say, that as agriculture and its kindred branches—horticulture and stock raising—should and must constitute the chief pursuits of the great majority of our people, every means in our power should be adopted to foster and encourage them. Even now they have every inducement to increased care and exertions in those directions. Markets are now brought to our very doors, or soon will be by extension of railroads, the increase of travel through our Territory, and the teeming population that moves with resistless activity around our borders. Everything that we can produce beyond our own consumption is, and w ll continue to be, in demand.

The country which we possess, the homes we occupy, are our own and the heritage of our children, by every right known and respected of men. Let us diligently improve and use them, remembering our own responsibility in the premises, and the duty we owe to those who may come after us. Even the log cabin is more stable than the lodge set up with poles and covered with straw and buffalo hides. The people who have homes and cultivated fields and orchards, are more secure from intrusion and aggression than those who have no fixed residence or abiding place. Here is our only home, and in it we must thrive and increase or dwindle and perish. Either result is largely within our own control. As we choose to have it, so will it be.

CONSTITUTION

OF THE

INDIAN TERRITORY.

B.

WHEREAS, The people of the nations of Indians inhabiting the Indian Territory, have agreed by treaty with the Government of the United States, and been by its agents invited, to meet in general council under the formes prescribed by the treaties of 1866, and the action thereon of the Government of the United States, having thus met to frame the laws and arrange the machinery of a government for the country occupied and owned by them, in order to draw themselves together in a closer bond of union, for the better protection of their rights, the improvement of themselves, and the preservation of their race, and relying on the guidance and favor of Almighty God to carry out in a consistent and practicable form the provisions of said treaties at the earliest practicable day, do hereby enact and promulgate the following as the constitution or organic law of the said Indian Territory:

ARTICLE I.

SECTION 1. All that portion of country bounded on the east by the States of Arkansas and Missouri, on the north by the State of Kansas, on the west by the Territory of New Mexico and the State of Texas, and on the south by the State of Texas, which has been set apart and guaranteed by the treaties and laws of the United States as a permanent home for the Indians therein lawfully resident, or such as may be in like manner settled therein hereafter for the purposes of this constitution, shall be known and styled as "The Indian Territory."

SEC. 2. Each of the nations of Indians who by themselves, or through their representatives, may enter this confederacy, do agree that the citizens of each and every one of said nations shall have the same rights of transit, commerce, trade, or exchange in any of said nations as he has in his own, subject only to consistency with existing treaty stipulations with the United States and the laws regulating trade and intercourse, and under such judicial regulations as are hereinafter provided.. But no right of property or lands, or funds owned by any one nation, shall be in any manner invaded by citizens of another nation; and it is hereby distinctly affirmed that the rights of each of these nations to its lands, funds and all other property, shall remain the sole and distinct property of such nation. Any Indian nation now represented in this general council, or which may hereafter enter in a legal manner, or be now in said Indian Territory, may be admitted to representation and all the privileges of this joint government, by accepting and agreeing, through their proper authorities, to the provisions of this constitution.

ARTICLE II.

SEC. 1. The powers of this government shall be divided into three distinct departments, to be called the Legislative, the Executive. and the Judicial, Departments of the Indian Territory.

SEC. 2. No person belonging to one of these departments shall exercise any of the powers properly belonging to either of the others, except in the cases hereinafter expressly directed or permitted.

ARTICLE III.

SEC. 1. The legislative power shall be vested in a General Assembly, which shall consist of a Senate and House of Representatives ; and the style of their acts shall be "Be it enacted," or, "Be it resolved by the General Assembly of the Indian Territory."

SEC. 2. The Senate shall consist of one member from each nation whose population is two thousand citizens, and one member for every additional two thousand citizens or fraction greater than one thousand : *Provided*, nations with populations less than two thousand may unite and be represented in the same ratio ; *And provided further*, that the Ottawas, Peorias, and Quapaws, shall be entitled to one Senator ; and the Senecas, Wyandottes and Shawnees to one Senator ; and the Sac and Foxes to one Senator.

SEC. 3. No person shall be eligible to a seat in the General Assembly, but a *bona fide* citizen of the nation which he represents, and who shall have attained to the age of twenty-five years.

SEC. 4. The House of Representatives shall consist of one member from each nation, and an additional member for each one thousand citizens, or fraction thereof, greater than five hundred.

SEC. 5. The members of the Senate and House of Representatives shall be elected by the qualified voters of their respective nations, according to their laws or customs, and shall hold their office for the term of two years. Vacancies that may occur shall be filled in like manner.

SEC. 6. The Senate, when assembled, shall choose a President and its other officers, and the House of

Representatives a Speaker and other officers; and each shall judge of the qualifications and returns of its own members. A majority of each house shall constitute a quorum to do business, but a smaller number may adjourn from day to day and compel the attendance of absent members, in such manner and under such penalties as each house may provide.

SEC. 7. Each branch of the General Assembly shall keep a journal and determine the rules of its proceedings, punish a member for disorderly behavior, and with the concurrence of two-thirds, expel a member, but not a second time for the same offence.

SEC. 8. The General Assembly shall have power to legislate upon all subjects and matters pertaining to the intercourse and relations of the nations of the Indian Territory, the arrest and extradition of criminals escaping from one nation to another; the administration of justice between members of the several nations of the said Territory and persons other than Indians and members of said nations; and the common defence and safety of the nations of said Territory. But the said General Assembly shall not legislate upon matters other than those above indicated. The General Assembly shall meet annually on the first Monday in June, at such place as may be fixed upon at their first regular session.

SEC. 9. Members of the General Assembly and other officers, both Executive and Judicial, before they enter upon the duties of their respective offices, shall take the following oath or affirmation, to wit: "I do solemnly swear (or affirm, as the case may be) that I will support the constitution of the Indian Territory, and that I will faithfully and impartially discharge, to the best of my ability, the duties of the office of ———, according to law. So help me God."

SEC. 10. The members of the General Assembly shall be paid four dollars per day while in actual attendance thereon, and four dollars mileage for every twenty miles going to and returning therefrom on the most direct traveled route, to be certified by the presiding officer of each House; *Provided*, no member shall be allowed per diem compensation for more than thirty days at any annual session.

SEC. 11. Members of the General Assembly shall, in all cases except of treason, felony, or breach of the peace, be privileged from arrest during the session of the General Assembly, and in going to and returning from the same.

SEC. 12. No power of suspending the laws of this Territory shall be exercised unless by the General Assembly or its authority. No retrospective law, nor any law impairing the obligation of contracts, shall be passed.

SEC. 13. Whenever the General Assembly shall deem it necessary to provide means to support the Government of the Indian Territory, it shall have power to do so; but no revenue shall be raised not actually necessary and in accordance with law, uniform in its operations throughout the Territory.

SEC. 14. All bills making appropriations shall originate in the House of Representatives; but the Senate may propose amendments or reject the same. All other bills may originate in either branch, subject to the concurrence or rejection of the other.

SEC. 15. The House of Representatives shall have the sole power of impeaching. All impeachments shall be tried by the Senate. When sitting for that purpose, the Senators shall be on oath or affirmation, and shall be presided over by the Chief Justice, and no person shall be convicted without the concurrence of two-thirds of the members present.

SEC. 16. The Governor, and all civil officers, shall be liable to impeachment for any misdemeanor in office; but judgment in such cases shall not extend farther than removal from office and disqualification to hold any office of honor, trust or profit, under this Government; but the party, whether convicted or acquitted, shall nevertheless be liable to indictment, trial and punishment according to law, as in other cases.

SEC. 17. The salaries of all officers created under this constitution, not otherwise provided, shall be regulated by law, but no increase or diminution shall be made in the same during the term for which said officers may have been elected or appointed.

ARTICLE IV.

SEC. 1. The Executive power of this Territory shall be vested in a Governor, who shall be styled the Governor of the Indian Territory, and whose term of service shall be two years, and until his successor shall have been elected and qualified. He shall be elected by the qualified electors of each nation, on the first Wednesday in April, at the usual places of holding elections of the several nations. The returns of the election of Governor shall be sealed up and directed to the Secretary of the Territory, who shall open and publish them in the presence of the Senate and House of Representatives in joint session assembled. The person having the highest number of votes shall be declared Governor by the President of the Senate; but if two or more shall be equal and highest in votes, then one of them shall be chosen by the majority of votes by joint ballot of both houses of the General Assembly.

SEC. 2. The manner of conducting and determining contested elections shall be directed by law.

SEC. 3. No person shall be eligible to the office of Governor who shall not have attained to the age of thirty years.

SEC. 4. Whenever the office of Governor shall become vacant by death, resignation, removal from office or otherwise, the President of the Senate shall execise the office until another Governor shall be duly qualified. In case of the death, resignation, removal from office or other disqualification of the President of the Senate so exercising the office of Governor, the Speaker of the House of Representatives shall fill the office until the President of the Senate shall have been chosen and qualified to act as Governor.

SEC. 5. The Governor shall receive at stated times, for his services, a compensation to be fixed by law, which shall be neither increased nor diminished during the period for which he shall have been elected; nor shall he receive, within that period, other emolument from the Indian Territory.

SEC. 6. The Governor shall, from time to time, give to the General Assembly information in writing of the state of the Government, and recommend to its consideration such measures as he may deem expedient, and shall take care that the laws be faithfully executed.

SEC. 7. The Governor, on extraordinary occasions, may, by proclamation, convene the General Assembly at the seat of government, to legislate upon such matters only as he may recommend.

SEC. 8. When vacancies occur in offices, the appointment of which is vested in the Governor by and with the consent of the Senate, he shall have power to fill such vacancies by commission, which shall expire at the end of the next session of the General Assembly.

SEC. 9. The Governor may grant pardons and respites, and remit fines for offences agains the laws of thist Territory, and shall cammission all officers who shall be appointed or elected to office under the laws of the Territory.

SEC. 10. Every bill which shall have passed both houses of the General Assembly shall be presented to the Governor; if he approve, he shall sign it; if not, he shall return it, with his objections, to the house in which it may have originated, which shall enter the objections at large upon the journal, and proceed to reconsider it. If, after such reconsideration, two-thirds of the members present shall agree to pass the bill, it shall be sent with the objections to the other house, by which it shall likewise be reconsidered; if approved by two-thirds of the members present of that house, it shall become a law; but in such case the votes of both houses shall be determined by yeas and nays; and the names of the members voting for and against the bill shall be entered on the journals of each house respectively. If any bill shall not be returned by the Governor within five days (Sundays excepted) after it shall have been presented to him, the same shall become a law in like manner as if he had signed it, unless the General Assembly, by their adjournment, prevent its return, in which case it shall be a law, unless sent back within three days after their next meeting.

Sec. 11. There shall be a Secretary of said Territory who shall be appointed by the Governor with the advice and consent of the Senate, and who shall hold his office for two years, and whose duties shall be prescribed by law. He shall also act as Treasurer of the Territory until otherwise provided. Before entering upon his duties as Treasurer, he shall give bond with such sureties as may be required by law. No money shall be drawn from the Treasury but by warrant from the Governor, and in consequence of appropriations made by law. There shall also be appointed in like manner one Marshal, who shall have power to appoint such deputies as may be authorized. There shall likewise be appointed one Attorney General and two District Attorneys, whose duties and terms of office shall be defined by law.

SEC. 12. All commissions shall be in the name and by the authority of the Indian Territory, and be sealed with the seal and signed by the Governor and attested by the Secretary of the Territory.

ARTICLE V.

SEC. 1. The Judicial Department of the Indian Territory shall be vested in a Supreme Court, three District Courts, and such inferior Courts as may be provided by law; but their jurisdiction shall not interfere with the civil and criminal jurisdiction retained to each separate nation by the treaties of 1866.

SEC. 2. The Supreme Court shall be composed of the three Judges, who shall be appointed by the Governor with the approval of the Senate, as District Judges. Two of said Judges shall form a quorum of the Supreme Court for the transaction of business. Their terms of office shall be six years, provided, that the office of one of said Judges shall be vacated in two years, of one in four years, and of one in six years, so that at the expiration of each two years one of said Judges shall be appointed as aforesaid. The Judge appointed for six years shall be the first Chief Justice of the Supreme Court, and upon the expiration of his term, the senior Judge in office shall be thereafter the Chief Justice.

SEC. 3. The Supreme Court shall meet at the Capital commencing on the first Mondays in June and December in each year. The Supreme Court shall be a Court of appellate jurisdiction from the District Courts, and original jurisdiction in such cases as may be prescribed by law.

SEC. 4. The Supreme and District Judges shall have power to issue writs of *habeas corpus* and other process necessary to the exercise of their appellate or original jurisdiction.

SEC. 5. The District Courts shall have original jurisdiction of all cases, civil and criminal, arising from the trade or intercourse between the several nations, and all cases arising under the legislation of this government as may be prescribed by law.

SEC. 6. Writs of error, bills of exceptions, and appeals may be allowed from the final decisions of the District Courts in such cases as shall be prescribed by law.

SEC. 7. It shall be the duty of the General Assembly to divide the Indian Territory into three districts, which shall be as nearly equal in territory and population as may be practicable, assign one of the three Judges to each district, and provide for the holding of terms of the District Court in each, at such times and places as may be deemed expedient.

SEC. 8. No person shall be appointed a Judge of any of the Courts, until he shall have attained to the age of thirty years, and be a person of good character and suitable qualifications,

SEC. 9. No Judge shall sit on a trial of any cause in which he may be interested, or in which he is connected to either of the parties by affinity or consanguinity, except by consent of the parties; and in case of disqualification of any Judge, the vacancy shall be filled as may be prescribed by law.

SEC. 10. All writs and other process shall run in the name of the Indian Territory, and bear test and be signed by the Clerk issuing the same.

SEC. 11. Indictments shall conclude, "Against the peace and dignity of the Indian Territory."

SEC. 12. Each Court shall appoint its own Clerk, whose duty and compensation shall be fixed by law.

ARTICLE VI.

SEC. 1. The General Assembly may propose such amendments to this constitution as three-fourths of each branch may deem expedient; and the Governor shall issue a proclamation directing all civil officers of the Territory to promulgate the same as extensively as possible within their respective districts, at least six months previous to the annual sessions of the National Councils of the nations parties hereto; and if three-fourths of such National Councils, at such next annual sessions, shall ratify such proposed amendment, they shall be valid to all intents and purposes as part of this constitution.

DECLARATION OF RIGHTS.

That the general, great and essential principles of liberty and free government may be recognized and established, we declare:—

SEC. 1. That all political power is inherent in the people, and all free governments are founded on their authority and instituted for their benefit; and they shall have at all times the inalienable right to alter, reform, or abolish their form of government as may be lawfully provided for.

SEC. 2. The free exercise of religious worship, and serving God without distinction of creed, shall forever be enjoyed within the limits of this Territory: *Provided*, That the liberty of conscience shall not be so construed as to excuse acts of licentiousness or justify practices inconsistent with the peace, safety and good morals of this Territory.

SEC. 3. No religious test shall ever be required as a qualification to any office of public trust in this Territory.

SEC. 4. Every citizen shall be at liberty to speak, write or publish his opinions on any subject, being responsible for the abuse of this privilege; and no law shall ever be passed curtailing the liberty of speech or of the press.

SEC. 5. The people shall be secure in their persons, houses, papers and possessions, from all unreasonable searches, seizures, and intrusions; and no warrant to search any place, or to seize any person or thing, shall be issued without describing them as nearly as may be, nor without good cause, supported by oath or affirmation.

SEC. 6. In all criminal prosecutions, the accused shall have a speedy trial by an impartial jury of the district wherein the crime shall have been committed; the right of demanding the nature and cause of the accusation; of having the witnesses to testify in his presence; of having compulsory process to procure witnesses in his favor; of having the right to be heard by himself and counsel; of not being compelled to testify against himself, nor to be held to answer to any criminal charge but on information or indictment by a grand jury.

SEC. 7. All prisoners shall be bailable before conviction, by sufficient surety, except for a capital offence where the proof is evident or the presumption great.

SEC. 8. Excessive bail shall not be required, nor excessive fines imposed, nor cruel or unusual punishment inflicted; and all Courts shall be open, and every person, for an injury done him in his person, reputation or property, shall have remedy as the law directs.

SEC. 9. No person, for the same offence, shall be twice put in jeopardy of life or limb, and the right of trial by jury shall remain inviolate.

SEC. 10. No person shall be imprisoned for debt.

SEC. 11. The citizens shall have the right, in a peaceable manner, to assemble for their common good, to instruct their representatives and to aply to those invested with the powers of government for redress of grievances or other purposes, by petition, address or remonstrance.

SEC. 12. The privilege of the writ of *habeas corpus* shall not be suspended, unless the public safety should require it.

SEC. 13. All power not herein expressly granted by the nations parties to this constitution, are reserved by them respectively, according to the provisions of their several treaties with the United States.

SCHEDULE TO THE CONSTITUTION.

In order to organized the Government of the Indian Territory, and secure practical operation for the same, it is hereby ordained—and the provisions of this schedule shall be of the same binding force as the constitution, of which it is a part—that it shall be the duty of the Secretary of this General Council to transmit a duly authenticated copy of this constitution to the executive authority of each nation represented in the General Council, and to ask the acceptance and ratification of the same by the councils or people of the respective nations. Upon receiving from such authority, notification of its acceptance and ratification by National Councils, representing two-thirds of the population of the nations represented in the General Council, it shall be his duty to promulgate such fact, and to call a session of the General Council from the nations ratifying this constitution, at such place as the present session may designate for its next meeting. It shall be the duty of the General Council, when so assembled, to adopt such measures as may be necessary to secure the election of a Governor and members of the General Assembly, and to fix the time of the first meeting of the said Assembly, whose duty it shall be to perfect the organization of the Government of the Indian Territory, under the provisions of the foregoing constitution; *Provided*, That this constitution shall be obligatory and binding only upon such nations and tribes as may hereafter duly approve and adopt the same.

ENOCH HOAG,
Supt. Indian Affairs,
President.

G. W. GREYSON,
Secretary.

C.

OKMULGEE, M. N.,
December 17, A. D. 1870.

Your committee to whom was referred, by resolution of the General Council of September 30, 1870, the subject of the populations and educational interests of the several nations represented in the General Council, report as follows:

The committee have no means of ascertaining the exact population of the several nations, and therefore are compelled to give it approximately from the information they have been able to obtain; and in their opinion it will exceed the figures given below.

The advancement in education has been seriously retarded by the late war. It closed, during its continuance, all the schools, and having destroyed nearly all the property of the country, the first efforts of the people after its close, were directed to rebuilding and gaining a subsistence. In consequence, a large number of the youths have grown up without the advantages of education. In this respect, its injurious effects will be long felt. Your committee, however, are happy to state that the nations are now giving this important subject their earnest attention, as will be seen from the following:

THE CHOCTAWS.

Since the close of the late war, the Choctaws have been able to establish and maintain only neighborhood schools, but are supporting about twenty Choctaw youths, males and females, attending schools in the States. An act of the Choctaw Council in 1870, authorizes the reopening of two boarding schools, one for males and one for females. The amount annually expended in supporting these schools is about ($33,000) thirty-three thousand dollars. There are three schools in each county, making forty-eight in the nation. The teachers are allowed two dollars per month for each pupil in attendance. The number of pupils attending school is (1,460) one thousand four hundred and sixty. The population of the Choctaw Nation is between sixteen and seventeen thousand.

CHEROKEES.

The population of the Cherokee Nation at the present time, cannot be accurately reported. The National Council during its session last year, passed a law by which a large number of those recently arrived from North Carolina and other States, are required to substantiate their rights before the Supreme Court now in session for that purpose, previous to their enrollment as *bona fide* citizens.

The census of the Cherokee Nation, taken previous to November 1st of the present year, shows the population to be about (17,000) seventeen thousand, including those cited before the Supreme Court as stated above, as to whose rights there is no doubt.

The school and orphan funds consists of the interest accruing on moneys invested in State and United States stocks.

For school fund, - - - -	$596,140.75
For orphan fund, - - - - -	219,774.00

Bearing interest at from 5 to 7 per cent. Interest about ($43,000) forty-three thousand dollars. The Cherokees have in operation (48) forty-eight district schools, three of which are for colored children, supported out of this fund, besides a few private schools in neighborhoods situated inconvenient to public schools. The public schools are under the supervision of a Superintendent, who is a native, and whose duties are defined by law. A large number, perhaps three-fourths, of the teachers are natives and paid out of the school fund, ($400) four hundred dollars each per scholastic year of ten months. Total number of scholars attending school is (1,928] one thousand nine hundred and twenty-eight. The orphans attending schools are boarded and clothed out of the orphan fund, which is only applied to those who are indigent and destitute. There is also one mission school under the control of Moravian Board. Previous to the war there was, in successful operation, two high schools or seminaries, one male and one female. The buildings are now undergoing thorough repairs, for the purpose of putting them in operation again. Each will accommodate about one hundred students, together with the necessary teachers and servants.

MUSKOKEES.

The population of the Muskokee Nation is about thirteen thousand, inclusive of freedmen.

The Muskokees have now in successful operation twenty-two public schools, located in different parts of the country, and under the supervision of a Superintendent of Public Instruction, who is a native. These schools are taught by one teacher each, with a salary of ($400) four hundred dollars for scholastic year of ten months. The last National Council created nine additional schools, which are now being put in operation. In addition to these schools, there is one boarding school in successful operation, accommodating eighty pupils, and one building under way which will be completed by spring, and will accommodate as many. These boarding schools are supported by the nation, except the salaries of the Superintendent and necessary teachers, which are paid by the boards of the Methodist and Presbyterian denominations, under whose control they are. The course of instruction pursued in the public and boarding schools, is as follows: commencing with the alphabet and its combinations into syllables, and extending through the various elementary branches as reading, spelling, writing, geography, grammar, and arithmetic. Six of the public schools are appropriated for the exclusive use of the freedmen of the Muskokee Nation.

Annual school fund from treaty stipulations, - - - - - - - -	$10,000
School fund contingent on the will of the president, - - - - - -	1,000
School fund from national appropriations, annually, - - - - - -	13,758
Total school fund expended, -	$24,758

The average number of children in attendance at school at the close of the scholastic year, ending June 30th, 1870, was about (700) seven hundred.

SEMINOLES.

The population of the Seminole nation is about (2,500) twenty-five hundred. By an act of the Council there has been established four neighborhood schools, which are now in successful operation, taught by efficient teachers, who receive an annual salary of six hundred dollars each. The whole number of pupils in attendance at school is two hundred and twenty-five, the average daily attendance at each being about forty. In addition to the neighborhood schools there is now in process of construction a mission building, superintended by the Rev. J. R. Ramsey of the Presbyterian denomination. The building will soon be completed and be sufficient to accommodate more than fifty pupils. By treaty stipulation the Seminoles have and use, for the support of the neighborhood schools, twenty-five hundred dollars, being the interest on fifty thousand dollars held in trust by the United States.

CHICKASAWS.

The population of the Chickasaw nation is between five and six thousand. They have eleven neighborhood schools. The whole number of pupils in attendance is four hundred and forty. In addition to these they have sixty pupils attending schools in the States, the expense being paid by the nation at the rate of three hundred and fifty dollars each.

Amount appropriated September last for support of neighborhood schools, -	$29,000
For supporting pupils in attendance at schools in the States, - - - -	21,000
Total school fund, - - -	$50,000

The teachers of the public schools are allowed out of the school fund three dollars per month for each pupil.

OSAGES.

The Osages have (50) fifty children attending the Catholic Mission school. The annual school fund is three thousand dollars. They have recently come into the Territory, and are not yet fully settled. They are beginning life anew, and it is hoped with better prospects of advancement in education than they have heretofore enjoyed. Their population is between three and four thousand.

CONFEDERATED PEORIAS, ETC.

The last census of Confederated Peorias shows the population to be one hundred and seventy. They have one school located among them, having been in operation about two months. Number of children attending school is about twenty-five. The school fund is the interest on from thirty-five to forty thousand dollars, invested fund.

OTTAWAS.

The Ottawas have a provision for education in their treaty of 1862—setting apart 20,000 acres of their land for the support of schools, and one section for school buildings. This land is near the city of Ottawa, and is valuable. They number one hundred and seventy-five souls, and have a school in successful operation of fifty-two scholars.

Population of	Shawnees, - - -	80
"	Wyandottes, - -	160
"	Senecas, - - - - -	188

These tribes have no schools among them.

SACS AND FOXES.

The Sacs and Foxes number about seven hundred, and have a school fund stipulated by treaty, amounting to five thousand dollars annually.

QUAPAWS.

The Quapaws number two hundred and thirty-six souls. No school fund reported.

Your committee are informed that measures are in progress for opening schools at an early day among the Quapaws, Senecas, Wyandottes, Osages, Sacs and Foxes, and Absentee Shawnees. The latter numbering about six hundred souls.

From the foregoing, your committee find the population of nations represented in the General Council to be about (60,000) sixty thousand ; number of schools, one hundred and forty; pupils attending school in the Territory and in the States, (4,800) four thousand eight hundred; amount of school fund expended annually in support of schools is about ($163,000) one hundred and sixty-three thousand dollars.

In conclusion, your committee would state that in their opinion nothing now so much retards educational advancement of the people of the Territory as their want of confidence in the permanency of their political institutions, growing out of the constant agitation, in and out of Congress, of the question of extending over these nations a territorial form of government, created by Congressional enactment. It is not necessary for your committee to state that the measure is utterly repugnant to every Indian in the Territory; but cheered by the words of hope from the representatives of the Government of the United States visiting us during the present session of the General Council, and imposing full confidence in the distinguished head of that great nation, we are led to believe that a brighter day is dawning upon the Indian.

The government proposed by the General Council—to be established over the Indian Territory—to be administered by Indians for themselves—is one founded on and growing out of treaty relations with the United States, and depends for its perpetuity not upon armies and navies, but upon the honor and good faith of that Government. It must be defended by the patriotism and intelligence of its sons.

JAMES M. C. SMITH,
Chairman Com. on Education.